CHARLESTON COUNTY LIBRARY

Little People, BIG DREAMS™
DAVID HOCKNEY

Written by
Maria Isabel Sánchez Vegara

Illustrated by
Ana Albero

Frances Lincoln
Children's Books

In the city of Bradford, England, lived a boy called David. He had three brothers, one sister, and two curious eyes that saw things in their own way. He loved drawing and doodling on the edges of his parents' newspapers and magazines.

His teacher thought he was a bright student with a promising future. Yet David already knew what he wanted to do in life! Sometimes he failed his exams on purpose, just to make everyone believe that he was only good at making art.

He was sixteen when he announced that he would go to art school. His mother worried he would end up failing, but David proved her wrong. He worked from sunrise to sunset for four years, learning the secrets of classic painting.

Back then, many gay people couldn't love who they wanted to and hid their feelings, but David refused to do so. He had always liked art and boys! He moved to London to study at the Royal College of Art, where he felt free to be himself.

David wanted to paint what he saw as beautiful, so he convinced his teachers to hire a male model for life-drawing classes. His name was Mo, and since everyone else was more interested in painting women, only David painted him.

He sold his first painting at a young artists' exhibition when he was still a student. It was a portrait of his father, and he was paid for it. It wasn't much, but it felt like a sign. Five years later, his first solo exhibition was a sellout.

David moved from England to sunny California. He was landing in Los Angeles when he noticed hundreds of pools blinking beneath him. It was like water and sunlight were playing together! Soon, these pools became his inspiration.

L.A. was everything he expected it to be, but three times better! His paintings were filled with the bright colors of pools, houses, and his friends. David took his camera wherever he went, capturing moments and bringing them back to life in his studio.

People loved his pictures of everyday life, and sometimes he even put himself into the paintings. Family and friends were the stars of his portraits, along with his two beloved dogs, Stanley and Boodge.

David broke new ground by painting huge landscapes, from the Grand Canyon in Arizona to the Yorkshire countryside near his parents' home. His largest picture was made of 50 canvases stitched together, and he donated it to an art museum.

Whatever he did as an artist, it was pioneering!
He mixed photos and films in his collages, designed
breathtaking stages for theaters, and even created
flowers on his tablet to wish his friends a good day.

For his 80th birthday, an exhibition took his lifetime of work across the world, from Paris and London to New York City, and thousands of his fans visited. Yet David didn't intend to stop working! There was so much more to look forward to…

And still today, he wakes up eager to share his colorful work with the world, because art is all about sharing with others. And as little David knows, nothing feels better than giving people pure joy.

DAVID HOCKNEY

(Born 1937)

1938   1950

David was the fourth child born to Kenneth and Laura Hockney in Bradford, England. Growing up, he admired the work of other artists such as Picasso and Fragonard. He had a passion for drawing and he knew from the age of 11 that he was going to be an artist. David moved to London in 1959 to study at the Royal College of Art. He was a brilliant student and totally unique; his paintings won prizes and were purchased for private collections. David often wanted to express his sexuality in his paintings through self-portraiture. At the time, being gay was criminalized, but he refused to be silent. His painting *We Two Boys Clinging Together* was one of the first nods to his sexuality in his art. David moved to Los Angeles in California, USA, and became known across the world for

1968   1973

iconic works such as *A Bigger Splash*. His style evolved and he created art using different mediums such as photography. In the 1970s, he worked on projects that involved set and costume design for the ballet, opera, and theater. Later, David returned to painting, primarily focusing on seascapes, flowers, and portraits of his loved ones. Always moving with the times, he incorporated new technology into his work by using fax machines and digital apps to create images. In 2018, his painting, *Portrait of an Artist (Pool with Two Figures)*, sold at auction for around $90 million, breaking records and cementing his place in art history. And today, David continues to amaze us all with his incredible art, showing that there are no limits when it comes to expressing yourself.

Want to find out more about **David Hockney?**

Have a read of this great book:

A History of Pictures for Children: From Cave Paintings to Computer Drawings
by David Hockney and Martin Gayford

 Brimming with creative inspiration, how-to projects, and useful information to enrich your everyday life, quarto.com is a favorite destination for those pursuing their interests and passions.

Text © 2023 Maria Isabel Sánchez Vegara. Illustrations ©2023 Ana Albero.
"Little People, BIG DREAMS" and "Pequeña & Grande" are trademarks of
Alba Editorial S.L.U. and/or Beautifool Couple S.L.
First Published in the UK in 2023 by Frances Lincoln Children's Books, an imprint of The Quarto Group.
100 Cummings Center, Suite 265D, Beverly, MA 01915, USA. T +1 978-282-95900 www.Quarto.com
All rights reserved.

No part of this publication may be reproduced, stored in a retrieval system, or transmitted, in any form, or by any means, electrical, mechanical, photocopying, recording or otherwise without the prior written permission of the publisher or a licence permitting restricted copying.

This book is not authorised, licensed or approved by David Hockney.
Any faults are the publisher's who will be happy to rectify for future printings.
A CIP record for this book is available from the Library of Congress.

ISBN 978-0-7112-8549-1

Set in Futura BT.

Published by Peter Marley • Designed by Lyli Feng
Commissioned by Lucy Menzies • Edited by Rachel Robinson • Production by Nikki Ingram

Manufactured in Guangdong, China CC112022
1 3 5 7 9 8 6 4 2

Photographic acknowledgements (pages 28-29, from left to right): 1. Volume 2, Page 115, Picture, 1, Artist, David Hockney, wearing his trade-mark hat and glasses, pictured in his studio, circa 1965 © Paul Popper/Popperfoto via Getty Images. 2. British painter, draughtsman, printmaker, stage designer and photographer David Hockney, at Rising Glen, circa 1978. © Michael Childers via Getty Images. 3. LONDON, ENGLAND - JANUARY 16: British artist David Hockney poses in front of his painting entitled "The Arrival of Spring in Woldgate, East Yorkshire 2011 (twenty-eleven)" at the opening of his exhibition David Hockney RA: A Bigger Picture in the Royal Academy of Arts on January 16, 2012 in London, England. The exhibition is the first major showcase of David Hockney's landscape work to be held in the UK © Oli Scarff via Getty Images. 4. British painter David Hockney poses at the Orangerie museum in Paris, on October 7, 2021, in front of his painting "A year in Normandy", a 91-meter-long artwork painted during the lockdown in 2020. - Hockney made a hundred drawings on iPad in a matter of weeks and captured the effects of light and climate change during the four seasons. © Thomas Coex via Getty Images.